This totally fabulous book is all about ME
and my very cool things, by:

Alexi.s

Illustrated by Simon Abbott
Written by Kirsty Neale
Designed by Chris Fraser

This is a Parragon Publishing book
This edition published in 2006

Parragon Publishing
Queen Street House
4 Queen Street
Bath
BA1 1HE, UK

ISBN 1-40547-582-X
Printed in China

My Cool Life

Introducing... ME!

My full name ....

My nickname ....

My address ....

....

My birthday ....

My age ....

Party time!

My star sign ....

The place where I was born ....

....

My hobbies ....

....

My favorite things ....

....

Stuff I don't like ....

....

Total angel!

My secret talent ....

My ambition ....

....

....

My Personality Profile

So what are you really like? Are you a Sporty Sort or a Brainy Babe? Try this quiz to find out.

1. What time of year do you like the best?

a) Spring—baby animals are SO cute!
b) Winter—lots of kissing under the mistletoe! Mwaaa!
c) Summer—so many cute hotties playing sports!
d) Fall—the best time to snuggle up with a good book!

2. What are you most likely to spend your cash on?

a) Duh! Chocolate of course.
b) The latest cool clothes and accessories.
c) Sneakers and trips to the swimming pool.
d) Books and funky stationery.

Yummy Choc!

3. Which of these animals do you prefer?

a) Dog
b) Cat
c) Horse
d) Rabbit

4. Which of the following would be a dream come true?

   a) Meeting your favorite boyband.
   b) Modeling cool designs on the catwalk.
   c) Scoring a goal for your basketball team.
   d) Winning a prestigious science award.

Results

Mostly as: Great Girl!
You're cheerful, loyal, and kind—
a brilliant friend who likes nothing
better than a good laugh.

Mostly bs: Funky Chick
You're seriously into fashion,
shopping, gossip, and parties.
A total trendsetter.

Mostly cs: Sporty Sort
Enthusiastic and full of energy—
you're a real team player who has
loads of pals.

Mostly ds: Brainy Babe
Hard-working and ambitious, you're
a super smart cookie, with a
wicked sense of humour to boot.

Me and My Family

Have fun scribbling about your family in this section.
Stick a picture of you and your family in the frame below.

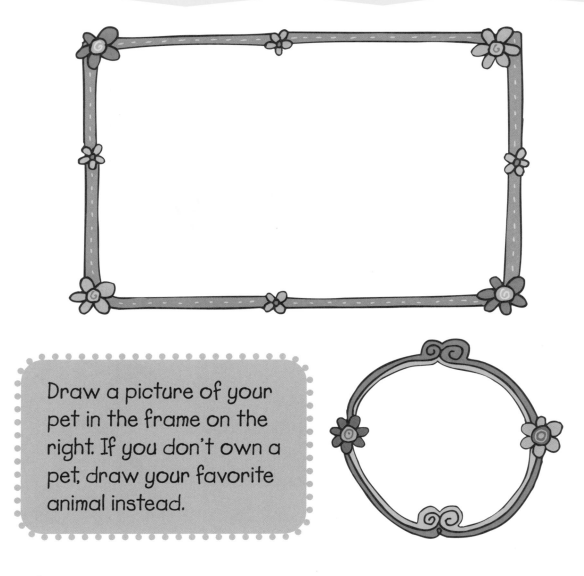

Draw a picture of your pet in the frame on the right. If you don't own a pet, draw your favorite animal instead.

The best thing about my family ....

....

The worst thing about my family ....

....

My most embarrassing family moment EVER

....

....

....

My dream family vacation ....

....

My favorite family memory ....

....

If I could make one person an honorary member of my family, it would be

....

My Best Friends

Such gorgeous girlies!

Stick a photo of your friends in the frames below, then write all about them.

NAME

NAME

NAME

....

....

....

The best thing about my friends ....

....

The worst thing about my friends ....

....

My most embarrassing friend moment

....

....

....

My best friend of all time ....

....

Special secrets about my friends

....

....

....

BFF (best friends forever)

My perfect pal-packed party ....

....

....

Stuff my friends and I like doing together ....

....

....

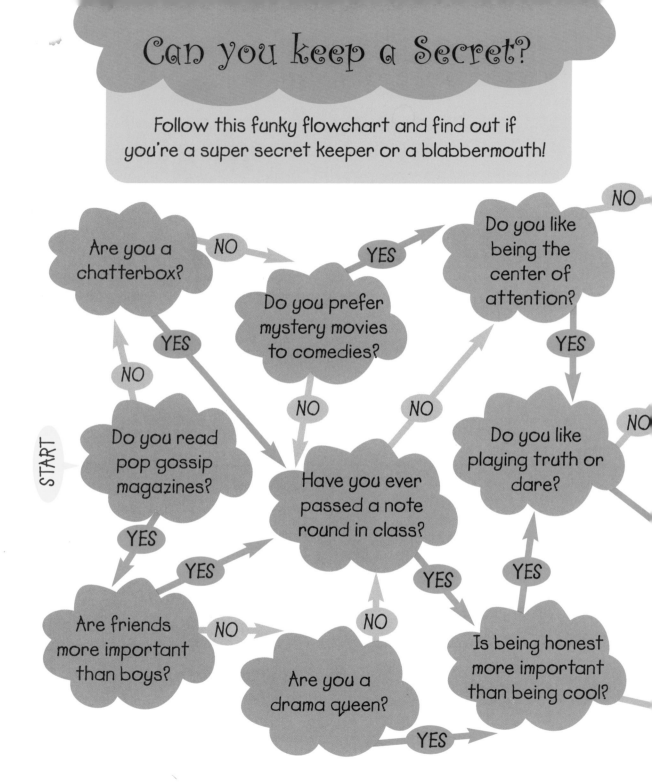

Are you good at organizing surprises?

YES → Do friends always take your advice?

Do friends always take your advice?
NO → Are you naturally nosy?
YES → Secret Keeper

Are you good at organizing surprises?
NO → Are you naturally nosy?

Are you naturally nosy?
NO → Secret Keeper
YES → Huge Hinter

Have you ever lied to your best friend?
NO → Are you naturally nosy?
YES → Have you ever started a rumor?

Have you ever started a rumor?
NO → Huge Hinter
YES → Blabbermouth

Do you often argue with your friends?
YES → Have you ever lied to your best friend?
NO → Have you ever lied to your best friend?
YES → Have you ever started a rumor?

Secret Keeper:
Wow. Your lips really are sealed! Your friends know you always keep their secrets, so they confide in you all the time. What a fab friend! Well done.

Huge Hinter:
You're not too bad at keeping secrets, but you find it hard. Just remember, dropping big hints is just as bad as telling all, so keep quiet.

Blabbermouth:
Being open and honest is great if a secret is yours to share. Otherwise, you'll need to keep things to yourself if you want to stay popular.

Total Crush City

I have a crush on
....
....

My dream date
is.......................
....

My perfect pop
boyfriend is
....
....

Want to discover your dating destiny? Simply set this page down flat and think of who you have a crush on. Then flip a candy over the wheel of fortune (below) and read the section it lands on to reveal your fate. If your candy lands in the center, flip it again and have another go.

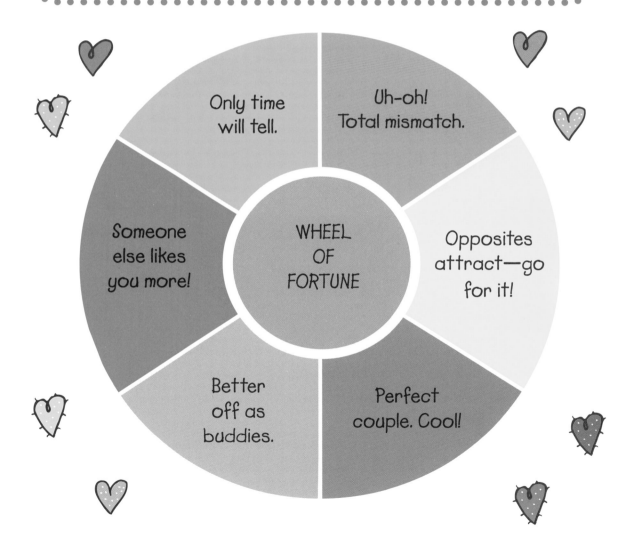

Only time will tell.

Uh-oh! Total mismatch.

Someone else likes you more!

WHEEL OF FORTUNE

Opposites attract—go for it!

Better off as buddies.

Perfect couple. Cool!

Club Together

Cool Club

Starting a secret club with your mates is great fun. Follow these top tips to create a super secret club of your own:

★ Give yourselves a totally cool club name.
★ Get creative and make funky membership cards and badges.
★ Organize special club activities and excursions
★ Hold your meetings in a secret club location.

Magic Message

To make your club messages harder for outsiders to read, write your scribbles in invisible ink:

★ Use a cotton swab for the pen and dip it in lemon juice for the ink.
★ Then, write your message onto plain white paper.
★ As the juice dries, the message will disappear.
★ To read what's written on the page, the person who receives the message just needs to rub a warm iron over it.

Be careful with the iron!

It's not just written words that can be kept club-confidential; using your own special language means that girlie gossip can be kept secret, too. Try this cool language code with your mates:

★ Take the first letter from each word and stick it at the end.
★ Next, add an 'AY' sound. For example, 'CLUB' is pronounced 'LUBCAY' and the word 'SECRET' becomes 'ECRETSAY'.

Create your own language here!

Lubscay ockray!

Otallytay!

What's My Pop Personality

Are you destined to be a really wild rock chick or a pretty pop princess? Try this quiz to find out.

1. What's your favorite accessory?

a) Pink and red stripy panty hose.
b) A funky retro-style cap.
c) High-heeled silver sandals.

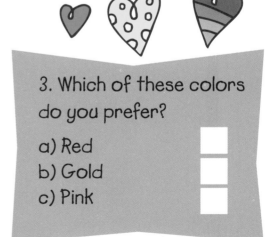

2. Which of these phrases sounds most like something you would say?

a) 'Hey, guys!'
b) 'What's up?'
c) 'SO cute!'

3. Which of these colors do you prefer?

a) Red
b) Gold
c) Pink

4. Who do you have a crush on?

a) No one—you see boys as mates NOT potential boyfriends.
b) The cutest-looking boy in your school, of course.
c) The same pop star as most of your mates.

★ ★ ★ Results ★ ★ ★

Mostly as—You're a wild rock chick!
You love loud tunes and guitar bands. Your unique sense of style and tomboy nature would make you a fantastic lead singer.

Mostly bs—You're a laid-back R'n'B babe!
You're a funky kind of girl who loves to get her own way. No one will EVER stop you becoming a solo superstar, girlfriend.

Mostly cs—You're a pretty pop princess!
You love wearing lovely, sparkly outfits and your mates are really important to you. You'd love to team up with them to conquer the sparkly world of pop together.

School's Cool

My school is called

....

I am in class

....

My favorite teacher is

....

I usually sit next to

....

My best subject is

....

My worst subject is

....

The school clubs and teams I belong to are

....

The most embarrassing thing that ever happened to me at school was when

....

....

My school is cool because ....

....

This is me, in my everyday school clothing:

This is me, dressed to go out with my friends:

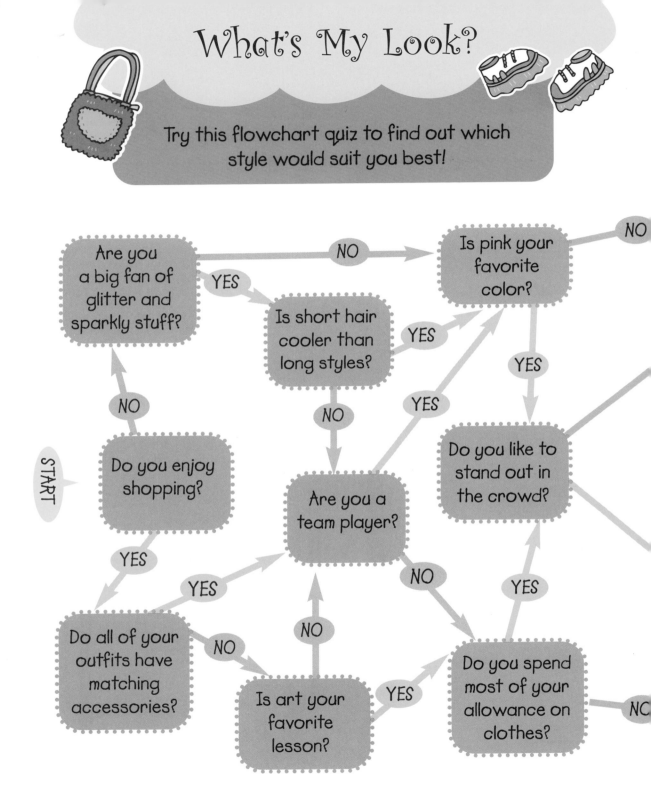

What's My Look?

Try this flowchart quiz to find out which style would suit you best!

START

Are you a big fan of glitter and sparkly stuff?

NO → Is pink your favorite color?

YES → Is short hair cooler than long styles?

YES → Is pink your favorite color?

NO → Do you enjoy shopping?

Is short hair cooler than long styles?

NO → Are you a team player?

YES → Are you a team player?

Is pink your favorite color?

YES → Do you like to stand out in the crowd?

NO →

Do you like to stand out in the crowd?

Do you enjoy shopping?

YES → Do all of your outfits have matching accessories?

Do all of your outfits have matching accessories?

YES → Are you a team player?

NO → Is art your favorite lesson?

Is art your favorite lesson?

NO → Are you a team player?

YES → Do you spend most of your allowance on clothes?

Are you a team player?

NO → Do you spend most of your allowance on clothes?

Do you spend most of your allowance on clothes?

YES → Do you like to stand out in the crowd?

NO →

Do you own more than two pairs of sneakers?

YES

Do you think that freckles are cool?

YES

NO

NO

NO

Total Tomboy: You prefer to wear casual clothes than trendy outfits. Comfort is much more important than fashion to a sporty girl like you!

Are pajama parties more fun than football?

NO

YES

Do you ever buy clothes from goodwill stories?

NO

YES

NO

Girlie Girl: You love to dress up and experiment with makeup and hairstyles. If it's pink and fashionable, it's in your closet!

NO

Would you rather be a fashion designer than a model?

YES

YES

YES

Can you sew?

YES

Cool Chick: You love fashion and style, but you'd rather make your own outfits than buy them. You are very creative and totally unique.

I finished this book about My Cool Life on:

....